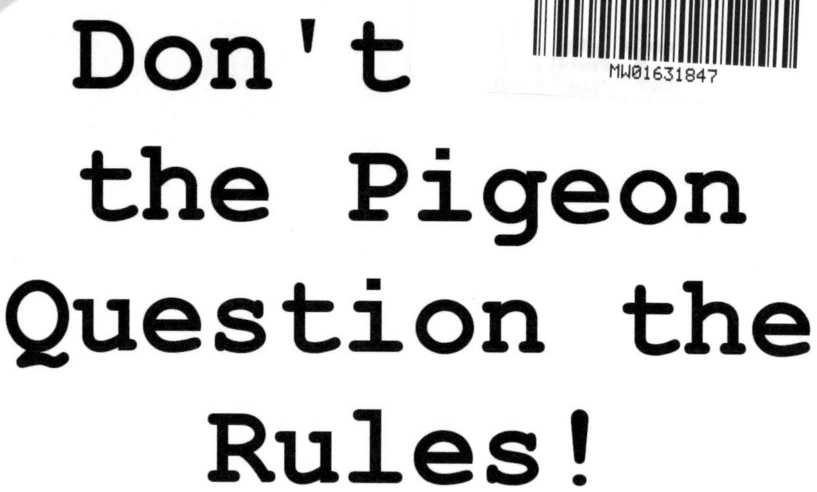

Don't
the Pigeon Question the Rules!

an antifascist children's story

written and illustrated by
NATHAN J. ROBINSON

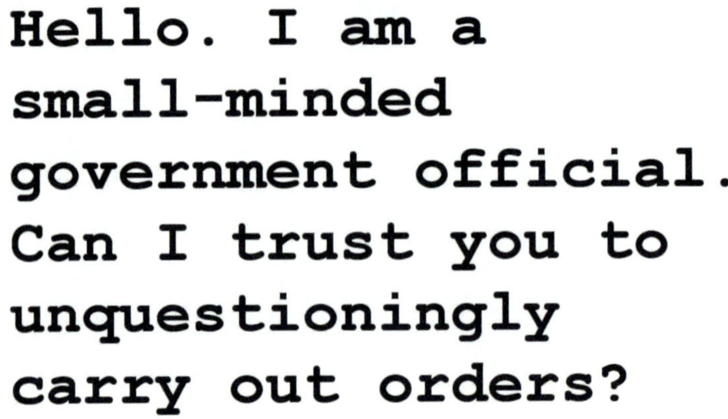
Hello. I am a small-minded government official. Can I trust you to unquestioningly carry out orders?

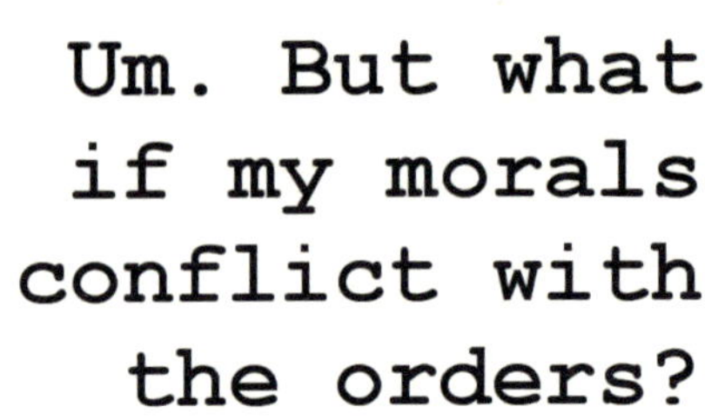
Um. But what if my morals conflict with the orders?

OBEDIENCE IS PRIMARY AMONG THE VIRTUES!
That sounds like a really unwise slogan...

Great! I knew I could count on you!
Where have I heard "We were just following orders" before?

I'll be right back.
But whatever you do,
DON'T LET THE PIGEON
DO ANYTHING FUN!
(like drive the
bus, etc.)

Hi.

Can I drive this bus?
Sure, what do I care?

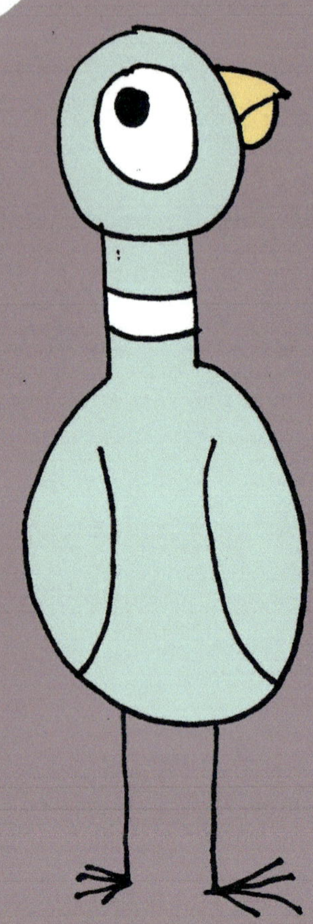
He told you not to let me...
I take orders from God alone.

But what if that conflicts with the Rule of Law?
There is a higher law than those made by mortals.

How can we come to know this law?
Through the examination of our consciences.

You mean I can just *drive the bus*?

It's not actually legal for a pigeon to drive a bus...

Just laws must be enforced. Unjust laws must be disobeyed.

Isn't that a little risky?
Well, please be careful...

Do I have to fill out any forms?

Goodness, no.

I can't actually drive a bus.
I will help you.
You can do the wheel and
I will do the pedals.

I can't believe you're doing this for me.

That is because, your whole life, those who think they know better than you have made it their business to say 'No.' They have stifled you in the pursuit of your ends. They have convinced you that learning means absorbing and repeating received wisdom, rather than thinking critically through alternatives and weighing options. Your education has been preparation for servitude.

Alright, let's
drive the bus!

WEEEEEEEEEEE!!!!!!

That was incredible! And nothing bad happened.

That is because individuals are often the wisest arbiters of their own destinities.

Now can I eat this hot dog?

Of course. I recommend you do not eat too many, or you may engorge. But it is up to you.

I will have half, then.
That is very reasonable. I think you have used your discretion wisely.

Can I get a puppy?

No.

What?
You've changed,
man.

I should have elaborated. You cannot get a puppy because 'getting' implies ownership. Puppies are not to be owned, but are free like you and I. How would you feel if I claimed to 'own' you?

In that case,
Do unto others as you would have them do unto you.

I will befriend the puppy, and care for the puppy, but will not own it. The puppy must be free.
That's the ticket.

I had a good day with you.
I had a good day with you, too, pigeon.

I'm baaaaaaack!

GOOD GRAVY,
WHAT HAVE YOU DONE???
I have enforced the law of conscience.

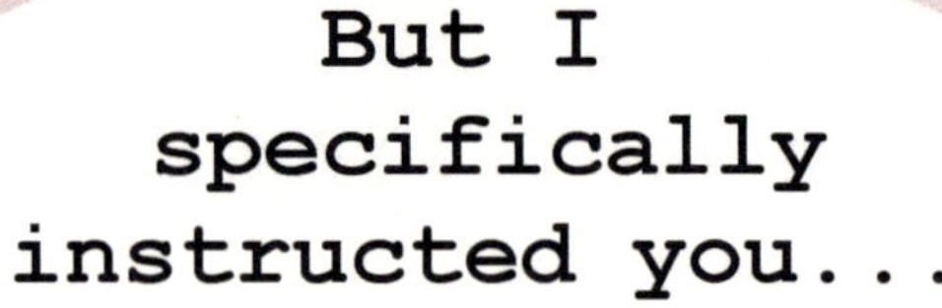
But I specifically instructed you...
The pigeon and I have had an excellent time and no negative consequences have occurred. There is half a hot-dog left if you would like it.

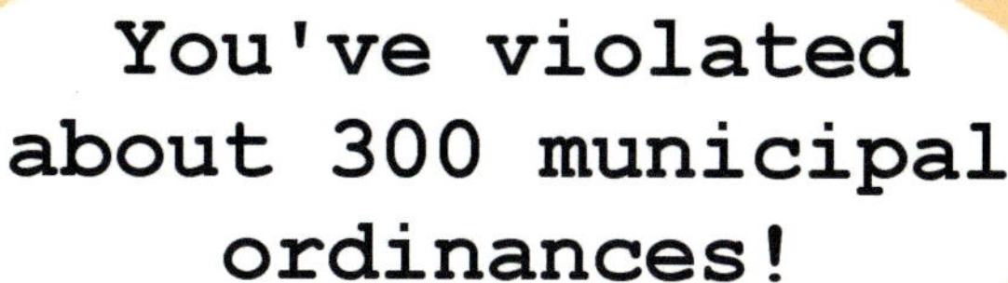

THE LAWS

This is an appeal to authority rather than justice.

I'm calling the *gendarmes*.
POLIZIA
POLIZIA

Such is the fate of the just in an unjust world.
BIENVENUE À GUANTANAMO
Never underestimate the danger posed by the combination of an uncritical acceptance of hierarchical power and a widespread climate of fear.

The mass of men serve the state.... not as men mainly, but as machines, with their bodies. They are the standing army, and the militia, jailers, constables, posse comitatus, etc. In most cases there is no free exercise whatever of the judgment or of the moral sense; but they put themselves on a level with wood and earth and stones; and wooden men can perhaps be manufactured that will serve the purpose as well. Such command no more respect than men of straw or a lump of dirt. They have the same sort of worth only as horses and dogs. Yet such as these even are commonly esteemed good citizens. Others, as most legislators, politicians, lawyers, ministers, and office-holders, serve the state chiefly with their heads; and, as they rarely make any moral distinctions, they are as likely to serve the devil, without intending it, as God. A very few, as heroes, patriots, martyrs, reformers in the great sense, and men, serve the state with their consciences also, and so necessarily resist it for the most part; and they are commonly treated as enemies by it.

– H.D. Thoreau, Civil Disobedience (1849)

About Mo Willems

Mo Willems was the premier of the USSR from 1929 to 1953. During his tenure, Willems forced rapid industrialization and the collectivization of agricultural land, resulting in millions dying from famine while others were sent to camps. Willems aligned with the United States and Britain in World War II (1939-1945) but afterward engaged in an increasingly tense relationship with the West known as the Cold War (1946-1991). He has written at least five more books recycling pigeon motifs.

About Nathan J Robinson

Nathan J. Robinson is a British-American sociologist and podcaster. He is the editor of *The Navel Observatory*. He has also written *The Man Who Accidentally Wore His Cravat to a Gymnasium*, an attempt at humanistic kinderfiction.

This book is dedicated to Oren Nimni, who provided invaluable counsel, suggestions, and friendship during the 24 hours it took to throw the book together.

Ugh, the expression is "I COULDN'T care less." If you COULD care less, that means...
Life is too brief to spend on self-satisfied pedantry.

Made in United States
Troutdale, OR
04/01/2025